This Is the Feast

Preparing for the Lord's Supper

Teacher Book

Dean Nadasdy and Thomas Doyle

CONCORDIA PUBLISHING HOUSE · SAINT LOUIS

3558 S. Jefferson Avenue, St. Louis, MO 63118-3968
1-800-325-3040 · www.cph.org

Edited by Rodney L. Rathmann

1 2 3 4 5 6 7 8 9 10 24 23 22 21 20 19 18 17 16 15

Contents

Introduction

For many Lutherans, their first Holy Communion may create a most lasting and meaningful memory. The taste of the bread, the scent of the wine, and the public character of the meal add up to an unforgettable moment. Yet none of these factors get at the essence of what happens in the Lord's Supper—a meal of forgiveness, unity, and peace through the body and blood of Christ.

Because the Lord's Supper is more than a memorable ceremony, the Lord calls us to special preparation. For example, Jesus carefully taught His disciples before He gave them the Sacrament. The apostle Paul admonished, "Let a person examine himself, then, and so eat of the bread and drink of the cup. For anyone who eats and drinks without discerning the body eats and drinks judgment on himself" (1 Corinthians 11:28–29). First Communion embraces more than a moment. It begins a lifetime of communion with Christ and His people.

This Is the Feast: Preparing for the Lord's Supper introduces young Christians, as early as fifth grade, to Communion and lays the foundation for a life of devotion. The sessions may be taught as freestanding classes but are best offered as part of confirmation instruction. To properly prepare for the Sacrament, students and their parents will survey both the Lord's Supper and Christian doctrine as a whole: the Law, the Gospel, prayer and worship, Baptism, and Confession and Absolution (see Luther's shorter preface to the Large Catechism, paragraph 2).

Through classroom participation and the "Taking It Home" sections, parents and guardians will learn alongside their children. Although parents may certainly ask questions and provide answers, they should not dominate class discussion. Parents should serve as mentors, support the class leader, and encourage their children to participate. This intergenerational approach affirms the primary role of family as the agent of Christian education (Deuteronomy 6:6–9) but keeps the focus on the children as learners.

Though *This Is the Feast* is designed as an eight-week course, you may use the materials for a weekend retreat. So as not to overwhelm the learners, schedule no fewer than two weekends of activity. That way, parents and guardians and their children will have adequate time to discuss the material for each session.

Congregations with larger classes may decide to divide their class into small groups of six to eight parents and children. Questions and answers could be discussed in small groups.

Session Structure

Each session in *This Is the Feast* follows the same structure. Here are the components you will find and the processes you may use:

Arrival Activity: In the sidebar, find activities to encourage families to participate in lesson-related activities as they arrive.

Prayer: Be sure to ask for prayer requests from the families present.

Key Verse: Following prayer, set the focus of the session by having a student read aloud the key verse.

Drama: Before class, assign the roles for the drama to class members. That way they will be better prepared to participate. Each drama includes a part for an adult, who can take responsibility for any rehearsals. (As an option, you could form a drama team to present all eight dramas for the course.) Questions for discussion follow each drama script. The leader may ask students and parents for their responses. If the class is large, you may want to divide into small groups for discussion.

Looking for Answers: Each session has questions that will be discussed by the class. This guide provides the answer to each question. You may wish to put each question and its answer into a presentation for computer or similar projection. You may wish to personalize the answers with narratives and illustrations.

What Do You See?: Have students look at the artwork and reflect on what they see. Use the discussion questions to guide them.

Taking It Home: Before dismissing students and their parents, remind them to use Taking It Home.

Listen to Memory Work: A memorization suggestion is included in many sessions. These may be recited or written at home for parents, with students reporting their completion of each assignment to the instructor.

Guidelines for Leading the Class

Be patient with children as they find Scripture passages and complete their notes. Invite parents to help. Everyone having the same version and edition of the Bible will allow the leader to give page numbers for passages cited.

Avoid turning the classes into lectures. As a leader, you should provide narratives and illustrations that not only clarify the truths being communicated from God's Word but also invite the learners to participate in communicating those truths. A basic guideline here: don't just tell students the truth of God's Word; through the drama and discussion, show them and then invite them to show you what they have learned.

Leaders should place a high value on keeping the children as the primary learners in the class. It may be easy to focus on adults and their questions. They're learning too! Some may grasp the beauty and deeper meanings of the Lord's Supper for the first time. Yet the class is designed for the children. Show caution, therefore, in responding too often to adult issues and concerns. And, again, encourage adults to allow the students to ask and to answer questions.

By all means, enjoy your teaching. You are privileged to welcome children into a fuller appreciation of God's sacramental grace, culminating in their first participation in Holy Communion. Be genuine with the class. Present these timeless truths with experiences and stories of your own. Your attitude as a leader will no doubt shape the attitudes of your class.

Session 1

The Law and Giving Myself a Test

Key Verse

Let a person examine himself, then, and so eat of the bread and drink of the cup. 1 Corinthians 11:28

Ask, **What do you think mirrors have to do with examining yourself before you receive the Lord's Supper?** Accept all responses. Then say, **Today we will answer that question. To begin our study today and each session, we will experience a drama. The drama today is entitled "If Mirrors Could Talk." After we experience the drama, we will discuss it.**

Have students and parents (or the assigned drama team) act out the play.

Before the session begins, place a large mirror in the front of the room. Or, if finances permit, purchase a small mirror for each student. Welcome participants as they arrive. Ask parents and their children to look into the mirror and write down what they see. When everyone has arrived, invite volunteers to share what they saw when they looked into the mirror. Accept all responses. You may want to say ***Tell me more*** *after a student has shared what he or she saw in the mirror. This will increase the quality and quantity of the students' responses.*

Pray that the Holy Spirit would strengthen the faith of the parents and children as they study together the truth found in God's Word. Then invite a volunteer to read aloud the key verse for today's session.

Drama

If Mirrors Could Talk

(NARRATOR [N] stands Stage R. Three players [M1, M2, M3] stand Stage L, facing the audience, each holding a large mirror. GIRL stands Center Stage.)

N: Once there was a girl who had three mirrors. These were not ordinary mirrors. These mirrors talked. The girl loved the mirrors because they always said something that made her feel good. When she didn't like how she looked, she went to her first mirror and asked,

GIRL: *(Moves to M1; stands in front of it)* Tell me, mirror, what do you see?

M1: I see a very pretty person.

GIRL: Pretty, you say?

M1: The prettiest of all.

N: And the girl smiled, thinking herself to be the prettiest girl of all. *(Girl moves to M2, standing in front of it.)* When the girl was feeling very guilty about having done something wrong, she said,

GIRL: I feel terrible. I shouldn't have done it.

N: And she looked into her second mirror with all her guilt, and the mirror said,

M2: Don't feel bad. You're a good person.

GIRL: Good, you say?

M2: The very best of all.

N: And the girl smiled, thinking herself to be very good, even though she had done something bad. *(GIRL moves to M3, standing in front of it.)* When the girl doubted herself, when she wondered if she could do what she had to do, she thought,

GIRL: I don't think I can do this. I am too weak. I'll never be able to do it.

N: She looked into her third mirror with all her doubt, and the mirror said,

M3: Yes, you can. You can do it. You're strong.

GIRL: Strong, you say?

M3: The strongest of all.

N: The girl loved her mirrors, all right. They made her feel pretty and good and strong. Yet something inside of her made her wonder if she could trust these mirrors that always told her what she wanted to hear. *(GIRL moves to M1.)*

M1: The prettiest. *(GIRL moves to M2.)*

M2: The best. *(GIRL moves to M3.)*

M3: The strongest.

N: She wondered about the mirrors that talked and if they could be trusted.

Discuss:

1. **Why do you think the girl loved her mirrors?** The mirrors told the girl only what she wanted to hear about herself. She loved to hear what they said because they affirmed her.
2. **Why do you think she wondered if they could be trusted?** The mirrors told the girl only what she wanted to hear. How could she trust whether they were telling the truth?
3. **What's wrong with only looking at the good in us and never seeing the bad?** Answers will vary, but may include that we will never know what we need to change; we will be led to believe that things are okay, when really they are not; it is not honest.
4. **How do you know if you've done something wrong?** First, we know from God's Word that we are all sinners. Second, we know we have done specific wrongs if someone corrects us or if our conscience bothers us concerning something we have done. Conclude by telling the students that God's Law acts like a mirror that shows our sins. Unlike the mirrors in the drama, the Law answers with brutal honesty.

Looking for Answers

This section lets students and parents explore what Scripture has to say about the concepts developed in the lesson. Studying Scripture and the chief doctrines associated with the Lord's Supper will prepare students to receive Holy Communion.

1. **Describe the three ways the Law of God functions in our lives. How is each important?**

   Curb—1 Timothy 1:9. The Law acts like a curb. It curbs outbursts of violent behavior.

   Mirror—Romans 3:20. The Law shows us our sin and that we are sinners.

   Rule—Psalm 119:105. For Christians, the Law acts as a guide for appropriate, God-pleasing behavior.

2. **Because God is holy and just, what does He require of every person? Read Matthew 5:48. How well have you lived up to God's standard?** God demands perfection. Jesus says, "Be perfect." Answers will vary. If honest, we each must admit that we are not perfect.

3. **If honest, what must we confess? See 1 John 1:8.** That we are sinners.

4. **What do we deserve because of our sin? Read Romans 6:23.** Eternal death because of our sin.

5. **What does God teach us in His Word concerning sin?**

   a. **1 John 3:4**—Everyone who breaks the Law sins.

   b. **Psalm 51:5**—We were sinful from birth, sinful from our conception. We call this inherited sinfulness *original sin.*

   c. **Romans 8:7**—The sinful mind is hostile to God. We sinners cannot and will not please God.

   d. **Galatians 5:19–21**—The acts of the sinful nature are sexual immorality, impurity, sensuality, idolatry, sorcery, enmity (hatred), strife, jealousy, fits of anger, rivalries, dissensions, divisions, envy, drunkenness, orgies, and the like.

6. **Why is using the Law as a mirror so important as we prepare to receive the Lord's Supper?** We need to recognize that we are poor, miserable sinners in order to realize our need for the forgiveness Jesus won for us on the cross. If we do not admit sin, we lie to ourselves and to God. If we confess our sins, God forgives our sins for Jesus' sake. Because we are sinners, we need to receive the body and blood of Jesus, through which we receive the forgiveness of sins.

7. **What does using the Law as a mirror show me about myself?** Answers will vary. If honest, we must admit that the Law shows us our sin and our need for a Savior.

8. **What do you conclude about yourself as you look into the mirror of God's Law?** That I am a sinner.

9. **Considering your conclusion, why is it important for you to receive the Lord's Supper? See Matthew 26:26–28.** In the Lord's Supper, Jesus provides us His true body and blood for the forgiveness of our sins.

What Do You See?

1. **What elements of this work of art indicate God's presence? See also Exodus 19:17–19.** God is too great and holy to be approached by man. In the Bible and biblical art, clouds, fire, and smoke often signify the barrier between Holy God and sinful man.
2. **What emotion are the people expressing in this picture? See Exodus 20:18.** The people were afraid in the presence of the holy and righteous God.
3. **Note the position of Moses in the picture, standing as the intermediary between God and His people. How does Moses in this picture remind us of Jesus?** Jesus is the ultimate intermediary between God and humanity. He came to keep God's Law perfectly in our place and to suffer and die to make us righteous before God.

The Ten Commandments

Taking It Home

Urge parents and students to spend at least 10 minutes during the next week discussing the following questions in order to personalize what was taught in the session. The study of Luther's Small Catechism will reinforce what students have learned from Scripture.

1. How is God's Law important to you?
2. How do you prepare for the Lord's Supper?
3. What do you receive from God when you eat His body and drink His blood in the Lord's Supper?
4. Share a time when going to the Lord's Supper was especially important to you.

Before the next session, students and their parents should review together Questions 74–78 in *Luther's Small Catechism with Explanation*. This will provide an opportunity to review what God's Word says about His Law and prepare them to study what God's Word has to say about His Gospel.

Close with a prayer thanking God for His Law, which shows us our sin and our need for our Savior.

Session 2

Grace and the Gospel

Key Verse

Therefore, since we have been justified by faith, we have peace with God through our Lord Jesus Christ. Romans 5:1

Say, **Today's drama is entitled "On Being Found." It tells the story of a young boy who receives an incredible gift from his great-grandfather. After we watch the drama, we will discuss it.**

Drama

On Being Found

(NARRATOR [N] stands Stage R; BOY with nicely decorated gift box [with envelope and letter inside] stands Center Stage. DAD stands Stage L.)

N: Once there was a boy who found a large box in his attic.

BOY: *(Holding box)* Wow! Now, this is really something! *(Shakes box and listens to determine what might be inside)*

N: Actually, the box sort of found him. Reaching high onto a shelf for an old baseball bat, he had knocked down both the bat and the box, and both had fallen right on his head.

BOY: *(Feels top of his head)* Wow! I can still feel it.

N: The box was beautifully wrapped in paper that looked very old. The box was very light, and the boy clearly had one thing on his mind.

BOY: *(Shakes box again and listens)* Wow! Gotta find out what's inside. *(Moves to DAD at Stage L)*

N: So the boy went to his dad and said,

BOY: Dad, look what I found!

DAD: How did you find that?

BOY: *(Rubbing head)* Well, it sort of found me. What do you know about this, Dad?

DAD: I know it was left for you.

BOY: Really? By whom?

DAD: By my grandfather, your great-grandfather. He told me to save it for you, for when you were old enough to appreciate it.

Before students arrive, place a cross in a gift box. Wrap the gift box with decorative wrapping paper. Have it in a conspicuous place so students and their parents will see it. After greeting parents and their children, ask them to write down what they believe is in the box. Then have them describe their favorite gift. When all have arrived, ask volunteers to share what they believe is in the gift box. You may want to list their ideas on a sheet of newsprint. Ask a volunteer to tell about the best gift he or she has ever received. Conclude the discussion session: **At the end of this class session, I will ask you once again to guess what is in the gift box. Today we will be discussing the greatest gift we could ever receive.**

Pray that the Holy Spirit would strengthen the faith of parents and children as they learn about the greatest gift of all. Then ask a volunteer to read aloud the key verse for this session.

BOY: So?

DAD: So what?

BOY: So, am I old enough?

DAD: I think so. Go ahead and open it.

BOY: Wow! Okay! *(Tears through wrappings, opens box, digs through old newspapers to find an envelope)* An envelope! It says, "To my great-grandchild."

DAD: Go ahead. Open it. *(BOY opens envelope, takes letter from envelope.)* What does it say?

BOY: It says . . .

DAD: Go ahead and read it, Son.

BOY: To my great-grandchild. You don't know me, but I am your great-grandfather. I died before you were born. But I asked your father to put this away and give it to you when you were old enough to appreciate it. I want you to know who you are and where you came from . . .

N: And the boy continued to read. He found out much about himself and his family—that his great-grandfather had worked seven years as a servant to raise the money to come to America. He learned that his great-grandfather was the first in his family ever to finish college. He learned that an inheritance had been set aside for him.

BOY: An inheritance? Can you believe this?

N: He learned that his great-grandfather had been a man of strong Christian faith who wanted his family to be rich in faith as well. All the boy could say was,

BOY: Can you believe this? I never knew!

N: He kept the letter. He called it his good-news letter. He was thankful for the day he found it, or, rather, the day when it found him. And when he needed to remember who he was and where he had come from, where he belonged and what he believed, he took out that good-news letter. He read it aloud again and again, and said,

BOY: Can you believe this?

Discuss:

1. **How is *grace*—an undeserved gift—evident in this story?** The boy did nothing to deserve the gift from his great-grandfather.

2. **How is the great-grandfather's letter like the Bible?** The great-grandfather's letter tells the boy of the inheritance that has been given to him. In the Bible, we learn of the inheritance that Jesus won for us on the cross. By grace through faith in Jesus, we receive this inheritance, which is forgiveness of sins and eternal life.

3. **Why did the boy keep saying, "Can you believe this?"** The boy was excited by the incredible inheritance he had received from his great-grandfather. The boy probably realized that he had done nothing to deserve this inheritance. Instead, the inheritance from the great-grandfather was given purely out of love for the great-grandchild he would someday have.

4. **How are we like the boy when we remember what Jesus did for us on the cross?** When we remember what Jesus did for us on the cross, we rejoice. We cannot understand how God could love us sinners so much that He would send His only Son to earth to suffer and die on the cross for our sins.

Looking for Answers

Using the Bible, direct students and their parents into God's Word. If the class is large, you may want to divide into small groups. This will give everyone an opportunity to share.

1. **More than anything else, what does God's Law show us about ourselves? See Romans 3:20–24.** Through His Law, God makes us conscious of our sins and our need for a Savior.

2. **Grace describes God's undeserved gift of forgiveness for sins and eternal life through faith in Jesus' death on the cross.**

   a. **What does God's grace tell us about God?** God loves us so much that He willingly sent His only Son to suffer and die for our sins.

   b. **What does God's grace tell us about ourselves?** God's grace tells us we are of great worth to God.

3. **How does God describe His grace?**

   a. **Romans 3:24**—God's grace caused Him to send His only Son to redeem us (buy us back) from our sin.

   b. **Romans 5:8**—God's grace is demonstrated in the fact that "while we were still sinners, Christ died for us."

   c. **Ephesians 1:7**—The riches of God's grace sent Jesus to redeem us from all sin. He has lavished His grace upon us.

4. **The Gospel is the Good News that we are freed from the guilt, the punishment, and the power of sin and are saved eternally from our sin because of Christ keeping the Law and suffering and dying on the cross for us. How is God's grace demonstrated in the Gospel?** We did nothing to deserve the forgiveness of sins and eternal life that Jesus won for us on the cross. Forgiveness of sins and eternal life are undeserved gifts from God.

5. **When we receive the Lord's Supper, we "proclaim the Lord's death until He comes" (1 Corinthians 11:26). Why did Jesus have to die? How did God demonstrate His grace in Jesus' death? How is Jesus' death Good News?** Jesus had to die in order to win for us forgiveness for our sins and eternal life. Point out that we call the day we remember Jesus' death "Good Friday." This Friday was not good for Jesus. But for us, Jesus' death is very good. Jesus did not deserve to die. We did. Instead, God directed His wrath (anger) at our sin onto His only Son. Jesus' death is Good News for us, for through His death, we are saved.

6. **The Bible uses many words to help us understand what God has accomplished for us by grace in Jesus Christ. Three of these appear in Romans 3:23–26. Read these verses. Then describe briefly what is meant by each word.**

   a. **Justified**—God declares the sinner "not guilty" because Jesus suffered the punishment the sinner deserved. Because of Jesus' death on the cross, God looks at my sin "just-as-if-I'd" (justified) never done it.

b. **Redemption**—Jesus paid the ransom for our release from death. In His death, Christ paid the price for our sins.

c. **Propitiation**—An atoning sacrifice that satisfies the righteous wrath of God toward sin. Jesus sacrificed His life for all sinners so that we could receive eternal life.

7. **The boy in the play exclaimed enthusiastically, "Can you believe this?" In the Apostles' and Nicene Creeds, we confess, "I believe . . . ." Why?** Compare the reason for the boy's enthusiasm with our confidence expressed in the creeds. When we speak the words of the creeds, we boldly confess what God has done for us in Christ Jesus. We say "I believe" concerning God the Father, God the Son, and God the Holy Spirit.

What Do You See?

1. **Describe the human emotion portrayed in this work of art.** Bleeding and nailed to a cross, Jesus, the Lamb of God, is suffering pain and agony as He sacrifices Himself for the sins of the world.

2. **What does Jesus' suffering have to do with you?** Jesus suffered and died for all sins, including yours and mine. Jesus took the suffering we deserve because of our sins, so that we might receive His holiness.

3. **Explain the concept of God's grace for us as illustrated in this picture.** God's love makes forgiveness, salvation, and new and eternal life available to us freely as a gift through faith. Jesus paid the price for this gift "not with gold or silver, but with His holy, precious blood and with His innocent suffering and death" (Luther's explanation of the Second Article). We don't merit or earn this gift; this is the grace of God.

With His holy, precious blood and with His innocent suffering and death

Taking It Home

Students should spend at least 10 minutes during the next week with a parent, talking about the following:

1. When in our lives have we experienced the grace of God in a special way?

2. What do Christians mean when they confess in the Apostles' and Nicene Creeds, "I believe . . ."?

3. Jesus said "Remember Me" when He instituted the Lord's Supper. What do you especially remember about Jesus when you come to Communion?

Urge students and parents to study the Apostles' and Nicene Creeds. Urge them also to study the questions and answers in *Luther's Small Catechism with Explanation* that discuss the three articles of the Apostles' Creed as a memory assignment.

Ask for volunteers to guess again what is in the gift box. After a few volunteers have guessed, open the gift box. Show the cross. Then say, **The greatest gift of all was God's sending His only Son to suffer and die on the cross so that we might receive forgiveness of sins and eternal life.** Close with a prayer thanking God for His greatest gift of all—Jesus.

Session 3

How God Gives Me Gifts

Key Verse

For in Christ Jesus you are all sons of God, through faith. For as many of you as were baptized into Christ have put on Christ. Galatians 3:26–27

Ask, **What great gift does Paul describe in these verses? When did you receive this gift?**

Say, **Today, our short drama is entitled "Come, Lord Jesus." After we experience the drama, we will discuss the questions that follow it.**

Drama

Before students and their parents arrive, write "Come, Lord Jesus . . ." on a sheet of newsprint. Greet parents and children as they arrive. Ask them to take a marker and write endings to the sentence starter written on the sheet of newsprint. When everyone has arrived, ask for volunteers to share what they wrote on the newsprint and why they wrote what they did.

Pray that by the power of the Holy Spirit working through God's Word, all may be strengthened in the saving faith and realize the great gifts God has given and continues to give to us today. Then invite a volunteer to read aloud the key verse.

Come, Lord Jesus

(MOM, DAD, JEFF, and ANN sit Center Stage at a table, facing the audience. The table may be set for dinner.)

DAD: Doesn't this look great? So who would like to say grace?

ANN: Let us pray. *(ALL bow heads.)* Bless this food, Lord, and bless our family. Thanks for the love we share and for the new TV You're going to give us. Now hear us as we pray.

JEFF: Way to go, Annie. I like that part about the TV.

DAD: You want to tell us about that?

MOM: Yes, Annie, please. I didn't know we were looking for a new TV.

ANN: Are you kidding, Mom? Have you seen the picture lately? And we only have a 32-inch screen. Everybody I know has at least a 50-inch flat screen.

JEFF: Little Annie here knows her TV screens.

MOM: So you thought you'd mention it in your prayer? You thought you'd thank God for it before you even had it?

ANN: I just thought that if I got God listening . . .

JEFF: He might start making things happen. I like that!

ANN: Which makes me wonder, Mom and Dad—why do we always say, "Come, Lord Jesus"?

DAD: You're changing the subject, Annie.

ANN: No, really; doesn't Jesus come anyway? Isn't He "where two . . ."—how does it go?

JEFF: "Where two or three are gathered."

ANN: Yeah, that's it. Doesn't He just come to every meal?

MOM: He does, but we say "Come, Lord Jesus" to let Him know how much we love Him, how much we'd be honored to have Him join us again.

DAD: Sort of like when we pray, "Thy kingdom come." He comes without our prayer, but we want Him to know that we'd be thrilled to have Him come right among us.

JEFF: Like in church, with the sermon. He comes there.

ANN: And the Lord's Supper. He comes there too.

DAD: Exactly.

ANN: So what about TVs? What about 50-inch screens?

MOM: That may be another story, young lady.

DAD: We'll have to leave that one to God.

JEFF: You gotta admit, though, it was a nice try.

Discuss:

1. **Why do meals and prayers seem to go together in so many families?** Mealtime is one of the times when families gather together. It is a terrific time to thank God for all that He has provided, including the food you are about to receive. When you say "Come, Lord Jesus," you are not only inviting Jesus to be present at your meal, but you are also acknowledging that He came once to earth to live, to suffer, to die, and to rise again to win for you forgiveness of sins and eternal life. You also proclaim that He will come again on the Last Day to take you to heaven to live with Him there forever.

2. **What does saying the "Come, Lord Jesus" prayer before a meal mean to you?** Answers will vary. See the response to question 1.

Looking for Answers

Discuss the following questions. If your class is large, you may want to divide into smaller groups so that everyone has a chance to share.

1. **How does God offer the gift of His forgiveness?**

   a. **Romans 1:16**—God offers His gift of forgiveness to all who believe in Christ Jesus as their Savior.

   b. **John 3:16**—God sent His only Son so that whoever believes in Him should not perish but have eternal life.

   c. **Ephesians 1:7**—Through the blood of Jesus shed on the cross, God provides the forgiveness of sins.

2. **The written and spoken Word of the Gospel and the Sacraments are the Means of Grace.**

   a. **How does the Bible describe the spoken and written Word of God? Read Luke 24:27 and 2 Timothy 3:16–17.** God reveals Himself throughout Scripture. All Scripture is God-breathed; that is, it comes from God.

b. **How does the Bible describe the Sacraments? Read Acts 2:38 and 1 Corinthians 10:16.** Peter says, "Repent and be baptized every one of you in the name of Jesus Christ for the forgiveness of your sins." Paul tells us that Christ's body and blood are truly present in the bread and wine.

3. **What does God provide to us in His Sacraments?**

a. **Acts 22:16**—Through Holy Baptism, God provides the forgiveness of sin.

b. **Matthew 26:28**—In the Lord's Supper, God provides the forgiveness of sin.

4. **Besides forgiveness, what other blessings does God give us in Baptism?**

a. **Titus 3:5**—God provides eternal salvation through Holy Baptism.

b. **John 3:5**—God provides us the Holy Spirit through Baptism.

c. **Romans 6:4**—God provides us a new life on earth and eternal life in heaven through Baptism.

d. **Galatians 3:26**—God makes us all one in Christ. We share unity in Christ through Holy Baptism. We are one family—the Christian family.

e. **1 John 3:1**—We are all God's children through Holy Baptism.

5. **When Jesus began (instituted) the Lord's Supper, He was celebrating the Passover meal with His disciples.**

a. **What did people remember when they celebrated the Passover? Skim Exodus 12–14**. The people of Israel remembered God's deliverance from Egypt and the cruel hand of Pharaoh.

b. **What do we remember when we receive the Lord's Supper? Read 1 Corinthians 11:26.** We remember the deliverance God provided us through His only Son's death on the cross.

6. **Compare and contrast the Passover meal and the Lord's Supper.** The Passover meal was celebrated to commemorate God's deliverance of His people from the bondage of slavery in Egypt. In the Lord's Supper, we celebrate the deliverance Jesus won for all people from the bondage of slavery to sin through His death on the cross.

What Do You See?

1. **How do the images down the center of the picture connect with the names we use when someone is baptized?** The artist shows the Father (cloud), Son (Jesus), and Holy Spirit (dove), the triune God in whose name we are baptized.
2. **Describe the expressions on the people's faces. What does this say about Baptism?** The people seem to marvel at the wonder of what is taking place. Though without sin, Jesus allowed Himself to be baptized as one aspect of His fulfilling of God's requirements in our place.

The Baptism of Jesus

Taking It Home

Students should spend at least 10 minutes during the next week with a parent discussing the following questions.

1. What family traditions do we have to celebrate holidays and special days?
2. What do you remember about my Baptism day?
3. What does it mean to you when you receive the Lord's Supper?
4. How does the Lord's Supper strengthen us as a family?

Before the next session, students and their parents should review the questions and answers from the Sacrament of Holy Baptism section of *Luther's Small Catechism with Explanation*. Parents may want to have their children memorize portions of the Holy Baptism section of the catechism.

Close by offering a prayer giving thanks for the means through which God continues to provide His gifts of forgiveness of sins and eternal life—His Word and Sacraments.

Real Presence

Before the class arrives, write in large letters on a sheet of newsprint, "A SPECIAL GUEST WILL BE VISITING TODAY." Greet participants as they arrive. Ask them to guess who the special visitor will be. Have students write their guesses on the newsprint. When everyone has arrived, say, ***It is now time for me to introduce our special guest! My father (or mother) has come to spend time with us in class today. Let me go get him (her).*** *Leave the room and bring in a photo of your father (mother). Speak to the photo as if you were speaking to your father (mother). Then ask,* ***Would anyone like to greet my special guest?*** *Share that it is ridiculous to believe that your father (mother) is really present when all that you have is a photo. Pray that the Holy Spirit would enlighten you this day as you study God's Word so that you might comprehend the magnitude of God's love provided in the Lord's Supper, as Jesus is truly present in this holy meal.*

Invite a volunteer to read aloud the key verse. Ask, ***What do you find amazing in this verse?*** *Allow time for volunteers to respond.*

Key Verse

Now as they were eating, Jesus took bread, and after blessing it broke it and gave it to the disciples, and said, "Take, eat; this is My body." And He took a cup, and when He had given thanks He gave it to them, saying, "Drink of it, all of you," for this is My blood of the covenant, which is poured out for many for the forgiveness of sins." Matthew 26:26–28

Say, **In today's drama, Jon and Molly are invited to spend a day in the presence of the president of the United States. You may be surprised at the turn of events that takes place in the drama. After the drama is presented, we will discuss it.**

Drama

The President's Presence

(JOEL is at Stage R near a stand or podium on which sits a large picture of the current president of the United States. MOLLY and JON are at Stage L. JON holds an invitation; one or both may have a camera. NARRATOR [N] may step in and out of the scene.)

MOLLY: I can't believe this! Read it again, Jon.

JON: You know it by heart, Molly. You got an invitation too.

MOLLY: Just read it. I love the sound of it.

JON: You are herewith cordially invited to spend a day with the President of the United States. He will be present with you from ten o'clock in the morning at the residence of Joel Schmidt. Please arrive promptly at ten for a day in the President's presence. Signed, THE WHITE HOUSE.

MOLLY: That's the part I like best—"a day in the President's presence." What time is it?

JON: Nine thirty.

MOLLY: We should probably head over.

JON: How Joel pulled this off I'll never know, but let's go.

N: Imagine an invitation like that! Wow, to spend a day in the president's presence! That's what Molly and Jon look forward to, but let's see what really happens. *(MOLLY and JON approach Stage R and stand as if at a door.)*

JON: *(Ready to ring doorbell)* Well, here goes.

MOLLY: Shouldn't there be security or something?

JON: Probably on the inside. Here goes. *(Mimes pressing doorbell; NARRATOR makes sound of doorbell.)*

JOEL: *(Mimes opening door)* You made it.

JON: We wouldn't have missed it.

JOEL: Well, come on in.

MOLLY: When does he arrive? The invitation said ten o'clock. I know we're a little early.

JOEL: Oh, he's here already.

JON: *(Doubtfully)* Really? Where?

JOEL: *(Returns to stand by picture and motions to it)* You're looking at him. *(Proudly, as if introducing him)* The President of the United States!

MOLLY: But that's not the president. It's just a picture.

JON: The invitation said we would spend a day in the president's presence.

JOEL: Right. Here he is.

MOLLY: But it's not the president, not really. It's not real. How can we ask any questions?

JOEL: *(Frustrated and holding up camera)* And who wants a picture of a picture?

MOLLY: It isn't the same, Joel. It just isn't the same.

N: It isn't the same, you know. A picture is not a presence.

Discuss:

1. **For whose presence are you especially grateful today? In other words, who makes you very glad because he or she is more than a picture?** Answers will vary.
2. **How is having a picture different from having a real person?** A picture is only a representation of the real person. It is not the real thing.
3. **What does it mean to you to know that Jesus is really present in the Lord's Supper?** Answers will vary.
4. **How is that different from Him just being represented by the bread and wine?** Jesus is truly present in the Lord's Supper. Explain that in the Lord's Supper, we get the real thing. Jesus' body is in, with, and under the bread. Jesus' blood is in, with, and under the wine.

Looking for Answers

Urge participants to explore what God's Word has to say about the Lord's Supper, especially concerning Jesus' real presence in the Supper.

1. **What are four names for Holy Communion? What do these names mean to you?**

   a. **1 Corinthians 10:16**—Body and Blood of Christ.

   b. **1 Corinthians 11:20**—The Lord's Supper

   c. **1 Corinthians 10:21**—The Lord's Table

   d. **Acts 2:42**—The Breaking of the Bread

2. **What did Jesus say when He distributed the bread to His disciples? See Matthew 26:26.** Jesus said, "This is My body."

3. **What did Jesus say when He distributed the wine to His disciples? See Matthew 26:28.** Jesus said, "This is My blood."

4. **What did Jesus mean when He said, "This is My body. . . . This is My blood"? Read 1 Corinthians 10:16 and also 11:27–29.** By these words, Jesus indicated that whoever eats the bread eats His body. Whoever drinks the wine drinks His blood.

5. **What do we still receive when we eat His body and drink His blood? What do we still receive when we eat bread and drink wine in the Lord's Supper? Read 1 Corinthians 10:16.** In Holy Communion, when we eat His body and drink His blood, we also receive bread and wine. In Holy Communion, when we eat bread and drink wine, we also receive His body and blood for the forgiveness of sins.

6. **We call this miracle "real presence." Jesus' body and blood are really present in, with, and under the bread and wine. How do we respond as we come into the real presence of Jesus in the Lord's Supper? (Consider the play read earlier.)** Answers will vary. We respond with joy, thanksgiving, awe, enthusiasm, and wonder at this magnificent gift.

What Do You See?

1. **What attitudes about the Lord's Supper does the artist express in the picture?** The disciples appear quiet and reverent, focusing on what Jesus is doing, and listening to His words.
2. **What might be the artist's intended message in focusing the disciples' gaze on the cup Jesus holds?** That the cup holds the blood that Christ shed on the cross for us for the forgiveness of sins. In a mysterious way, we receive Jesus' very blood together with the wine in the Lord's Supper.
3. **Look at the bread centered on the table. What does it foreshadow?** The bread is broken, just as Jesus' body was broken for us on the cross. In a mysterious way, we receive Jesus' body together with the bread when we partake in the Lord's Supper.

The Lord's Supper

Taking It Home

Urge students to spend time talking with their parents this week about the questions included below. Also remind parents and students to go over the questions and answers concerning the Lord's Supper in *Luther's Small Catechism with Explanation*. Parents may want their children to memorize portions of the Sacrament of the Altar section from Luther's Small Catechism or Bible verses that give greater meaning to the miracle that occurs when we receive the body and blood of Jesus in the Lord's Supper.

1. Whose real, live presence do you especially appreciate?
2. What do you think and feel as you come into the real presence of Jesus in the Lord's Supper?

Close with a prayer thanking God for showering us with His gifts, especially the gift of Jesus' body and blood in the Lord's Supper for the forgiveness of sins.

Session 5

Bring to class a helium-filled balloon tied to a string. Tie an object to the bottom of the string that will keep the balloon from rising. Greet parents and children as they arrive. Say to each family, ***I took this balloon out earlier to let it fly into the sky. Unfortunately, I couldn't get it to fly. Can you figure out how I might get this balloon to soar to the clouds?*** *When everyone has arrived, say,* ***It probably didn't take you long to figure out that in order for the balloon to rise, the weight must be removed from the string.*** *Take the balloon outdoors. Remove the weight. As you remove the weight, say,* ***It's impossible to soar when you carry a weight. Many people carry with them the weight of unconfessed and unforgiven sin. God invites us sinners, "Come to Me, all who labor and are heavy laden, and I will give you rest" (Matthew 11:28). God promises to lift the weight, the burden, of sin for all who believe in Jesus as their Lord and Savior. Through His life, death, and resurrection, Jesus earned our freedom from all that would weigh us down. With the weight of our sins lifted from us, we are able to serve God and others.*** *Pray,* ***Thank You, Lord, for sending Your only Son to earth to suffer and die on the cross for our sins. Thank You especially for giving us the Lord's Supper, through which You provide us forgiveness of sins. Strengthen us with Your peace as we study Your Word and receive the assurance that You have forgiven all of our sins.*** *Then, invite a volunteer to read aloud the key verse.*

Meal of Forgiveness

Key Verse

For by a single offering He has perfected for all time those who are being sanctified. Hebrews 10:14

Ask, **Ever feel guilty over something you did wrong? Guilt can really weigh us down. In today's drama, a girl is followed around by her guilt, which reminds her often of her sin. She looks for ways to get rid of her guilt.**

Drama

Guilt Free

(NARRATOR [N] at Stage R. GIRL and GUILT at Stage L. GUILT [perhaps dressed in black] stands directly behind GIRL and follows right behind her wherever she goes. FRIEND is offstage.)

N: Once there was a girl who was very guilty. *(GIRL begins to walk about; GUILT follows right at her back.)* Wherever she went, her guilt went with her.

GIRL: Oh, I know I shouldn't have done it. I was very wrong.

GUILT: *(In GIRL's ear)* You sure were. You were as wrong as wrong can be.

GIRL: So what do I do now? *(Stops walking about)*

GUILT: You live with it.

GIRL: It?

GUILT: You live with me, your guilt. You're stuck with me. Where you go, I go.

GIRL: *(Walks again; GUILT follows on her heels.)* I hate you.

GUILT: No, you hate yourself. I wouldn't be here if you hadn't done it.

GIRL: I know. You're right, of course. *(Still pacing, with GUILT following)* Maybe I should read a book. You know, one of those self-help books that will tell me I'm really just fine.

GUILT: I'll still be here. The kind of book you're after will never get the best of me.

GIRL: Well then, I'll just forget about it. That's it. I'll deny it.

GUILT: Won't work. I'll be on your back lickety-split.

GIRL: Lickety-split?

GUILT: I won't let you forget.

N: It isn't easy getting rid of guilt.

GIRL: I'll phone Susie. I love Susie. She'll tell me that it's okay and not to worry.

GUILT: I'll tell you that you can't trust Susie, that it's not okay, and that you're really a bad person.

GIRL: *(Stops with GUILT right at her back)* Then what happens next? Do I live forever with you on my back?

N: And that's exactly what she would have done—lived with her guilt forever—if someone had not come. *(FRIEND enters Stage L and walks up to GUILT.)* One who was stronger and greater than she. One who looked guilt in the eye and said,

FRIEND: Get behind me. You're mine now.

N: And sure enough *(GUILT steps behind FRIEND)*, the girl's guilt became his, and as he walked away *(FRIEND exits Stage L with GUILT at his back)*, he said with a face-wide smile,

FRIEND: You're free of guilt now. I'm taking it away. *(FRIEND and GUILT exit.)*

N: The girl stood still and looked over her shoulder, and she smiled too and said,

GIRL: I am guilt free. *(Smiles and walks off confidently)*

Discuss:

1. **In what way is the girl like us when we've sinned?** We feel guilty when we sin. At times, our guilt can really burden us. When Jesus suffered and died on the cross, He took our sin and our guilt with Him.

2. **What bad ways of handling guilt was the girl going to try?** The girl looked for many ways to get rid of her guilt. She considered reading self-help books, denying it, and calling Susie, a person she loved and trusted.

3. **How is Jesus a friend to sinners when considering our guilt?** Jesus took our guilt and our sin with Him to the cross. When He died, so did our sin and therefore also our guilt.

Looking for Answers

Discuss the questions that follow. If the class is large, you may want to divide into smaller groups so that everyone has a chance to share.

1. **What is the chief blessing of Holy Communion? See Matthew 26:28.** Forgiveness of sins is the chief blessing received in the Lord's Supper.

2. **Before Jesus died on the cross, the Jewish priests sacrificed animals daily for the forgiveness of sins. How is Jesus' sacrifice on the cross different from and better than these other sacrifices? See Hebrews 10:10–12.** Jesus' sacrificial death on the cross was a "once for all" sacrifice. Before Jesus' death, the Jewish

priests would daily sacrifice an animal for the forgiveness of sins.

3. **When we celebrate the Lord's Supper, is Christ sacrificed over and over again each time? See Hebrews 10:14, 18.** No. Jesus' sacrificial death on the cross was the one-time sacrifice necessary to win forgiveness of sins for us.

4. **How do you know for sure that your sins are forgiven in the Lord's Supper? See Matthew 26:28 and 1 John 1:7.** Jesus tells us that in the Lord's Supper, our sins are forgiven. How do we know? Jesus tells us so!

5. **What other blessings does God provide in the Lord's Supper? Read Romans 6:8–9 and 1 Peter 2:24.** God also provides the power to live our lives for righteousness (as God desires) and the power to withstand temptation. All this the Holy Spirit provides as our faith is strengthened in the Holy Meal.

6. **Consider how guilt followed the girl around in the play read earlier. Now read what God says about our sins forgiven through faith in Jesus' death on the cross. Read Psalm 103:12. How can you respond as guilt tries to follow you around, reminding you of past sins?** As far as the east is from the west—that's a long way—God has removed our sins from us. They are gone! Jesus took them to the cross.

What Do You See?

1. **Contrast the appearance of the son with the appearance of the father. What can this tell you about yourself and your relationship with the heavenly Father?** The son has ragged clothes. The father is richly dressed. We come before the heavenly Father like beggars.
2. **The father reaches out to welcome and embrace the returning son. How is this like God when we return to Him seeking forgiveness?** God willingly welcomes us when we come to Him seeking forgiveness. Jesus has earned forgiveness for all our sins.

Jesus Seeks the Lost

Taking It Home

Students and their parents should spend 10 minutes or more discussing the following questions:

1. When did we last share a word of forgiveness between us?
2. What makes forgiving someone so difficult sometimes?
3. What do we think about when we pray, "Forgive us our trespasses as we forgive those who trespass against us"?
4. What do I think and feel when I look at a cross and consider that Jesus sacrificed His life for me?

Urge parents to spend time this week discussing the preceding questions with their children. Also continue to study the question-and-answer section from *Luther's Small Catechism with Explanation* concerning the Lord's Supper. Again, suggest that parents give their children reasonable portions of the catechism or key Bible verses to memorize concerning the blessings and benefits received in the Lord's Supper.

Close with a prayer giving thanks to God for sending Jesus to take our sins and our guilt over those sins to the cross.

Session 6

Other Blessings Received in Holy Communion

Key Verse

The cup of blessing that we bless, is it not a participation in the blood of Christ? The bread that we break, is it not a participation in the body of Christ? Because there is one bread, we who are many are one body, for we all partake of the one bread. 1 Corinthians 10:16–17

Say, **This may be a tough passage to understand. Does anyone want to try to explain what our key verse means?** *Accept all responses. Then say,* **In today's lesson, we will learn that this verse describes an extra blessing received when we eat and drink Jesus' body and blood in Holy Communion.**

Before participants arrive, write on a large sheet of newsprint, "It's not polite to ask for more!" Greet parents and children as they arrive. Ask them to make a list of times when it is not polite to ask for more. When everyone has arrived, have volunteers share their lists. Say, **In today's lesson, we learn that Jesus gives us more in the Lord's Supper, and we didn't even have to ask for it!**

Pray that by the power of the Holy Spirit working through God's Word, we might joyfully and thankfully receive the many blessings God provides us in the Lord's Supper. Then, invite a volunteer to read aloud the key verse.

Drama

A Dinner Not Soon Forgotten

(ALL at Center Stage; MOM to the right of MARY and LISA)

MARY: So what was it like?

LISA: I'll never forget it.

MARY: I think you're the first person I've ever met who actually won a contest. Just think of it—dinner with him!

LISA: And I didn't even do anything to win.

MOM: Sure you did, Lisa. You filled out the entry card and dropped it in the box.

LISA: Wow, some real talent there. I mean, I didn't have to sing or write an essay or anything.

MOM: But you did win.

LISA: Someone drew my name out of a box.

MARY: Yes, a box with the names of thousands of other kids who wanted to have dinner with him. So are you going to tell me about it or not?

MOM: Tell her, Lisa.

MARY: What's he like?

LISA: He's everything I thought he would be—kind, funny, smart.

MARY: And handsome.

LISA: That too.

MARY: What did he say?

LISA: We talked about all kinds of things, mostly about me.

MARY: About you? He talked about you?

LISA: He asked questions, almost like he was interested in me—as a person, I mean.

MARY: *(Swooning)* Wow-w-w. So what did he ask?

LISA: About my family, our school, my friends, what I want to do when I grow up.

MARY: And you answered him? You talked to him?

LISA: No, I sat there slurping soup. Yes, I answered him.

MARY: Wow-w-w. What did you say?

LISA: A lot of things. Mostly "thanks," though. I think I must have said "thanks" ten thousand times. I mean, like, he was having dinner with me! It's something I'll never forget. I felt like I was there with every girl my age. He knew how I felt.

MARY: And when you said "thanks," what did he say?

LISA: He said, "You're welcome."

MARY: Wow-w-w. Wow-w-w.

Discuss:

1. **With whom do you think Lisa had dinner? Explain your response.** Answers will vary. Accept all responses.
2. **How is dinner with someone special similar to Holy Communion?** In Holy Communion, we have a meal with Jesus. Jesus, too, is concerned about our lives—family, school, friends, dreams.

Looking for Answers

Discuss the questions that follow. If your class is large, you may want to divide into small groups so that everyone has a chance to share.

1. **Besides forgiveness, life, and salvation, what other blessings does God give you in Holy Communion? Read Romans 8:10 and 1 Corinthians 10:17.** Jesus gives us victory over sin and hell and strength for the new life in Him. Also, we proclaim unity with other Christians who receive it.
2. **Read 1 Corinthians 11:26 and answer the following questions.**

   a. **What event will you proclaim or announce when you come to Holy Communion?** You will proclaim the Lord's death until He comes.

   b. **What event will you most look forward to when you come to Holy Communion?** You should look forward to the time when Christ will come again—Judgment Day—to take us to live with Him forever in heaven.
3. **Read 1 Corinthians 10:16–17. Diagram the circles of belonging—unity—in which Christians participate when they receive the Lord's Supper.** Diagrams will vary.

Although Christians are all different, they proclaim their unity or oneness as they receive the body and blood of Jesus in the Lord's Supper.

4. **In what ways will the Lord strengthen you in the Lord's Supper? See 1 Peter 2:24.** Jesus strengthens us with His body and blood to live in His righteousness.

5. **In what way(s) is Communion a meal of thanksgiving?** When we receive the Lord's Supper, we give thanks to God for the blessings and power He bestows on us in the meal. It is a celebration of the forgiveness of sins and eternal life Jesus won for us on the cross.

What Do You See?

1. **Describe the people receiving Holy Communion in this picture. What message is this illustration seeking to convey?** Answers will vary. The members of the congregation are males and females, younger and older, and represent more than one race. God desires to give the blessings of this Sacrament to all who receive it in faith.

The Sacrament of the Altar

2. **Explain the significance of going to the altar to receive the very body and blood of Jesus for the forgiveness of sins.** Jesus gave Himself as the once-for-all sacrifice for us and for all people.

3. **Note the cross on the altar. Where is the focus when we receive the Lord's Supper? Why?** Jesus is the focus of the Lord's Supper because, through His body and blood, He gives us the forgiveness of sins.

Taking It Home

Urge parents to spend at least 10 minutes with their children this week discussing the following questions. If time permits, suggest that parents review with their children the entire question-and-answer section of *Luther's Small Catechism with Explanation* that pertains to the Lord's Supper. Also, parents may wish to assign 1 Corinthians 10:16–17 for the children to memorize.

1. How is the unity you celebrate in the Lord's Supper important to you?

2. Who comes to mind when you hear the words "and with all the company of heaven"? Whom do you love in heaven who is praising God?

3. In your own words, try to answer someone who asks, "What's so special about Communion in your church?"

As the closing prayer, ask each family to give thanks either publicly or privately for the many blessings that God provides to His people in the Lord's Supper.

Table Graces

Key Verse

You prepare a table before me in the presence of my enemies; You anoint my head with oil; my cup overflows. Surely goodness and mercy shall follow me all the days of my life, and I shall dwell in the house of the Lord *forever. Psalm 23:5–6*

Ask, **What does this key verse describe?** *Answers will vary.*

Drama

Setting the Table

(MOM's voice is heard offstage. JAMIE is setting a table at Center Stage. A table with tablecloth and appropriate utensils may be used, or JAMIE may mime the action without props. MOM may carry a floral centerpiece.)

MOM: Jamie, do you want to try setting the table?

JAMIE: *(Setting plates)* I am trying to set the table, Mom. Emily Toast would be proud of me.

MOM: That's "Post," sweetie. Emily Post.

JAMIE: Right. *(To audience)* Emily Toast is some expert on etiquette my mom is always talking about. We're having a big dinner tonight. My brother's coming home after four years in the Air Force.

MOM: Two forks on the left, Jamie . . .

JAMIE: *(Setting silverware)* Knife and spoon on the right. Gotcha, Mom.

MOM: Spoon on the outside . . .

JAMIE: Salad fork on the outside left. Under control. *(Sarcastically)* Travis will appreciate it. *(To audience)* Travis is the flyboy home for good. Actually, I don't know if he'll even notice the silverware.

MOM: Yes, he will, Jamie. That's his great-grandmother's good china, and he knows it only gets used for the finest occasions. You set for how many?

JAMIE: *(Kiddingly)* Three hundred. Right, Mom?

MOM: Jamie.

JAMIE: It's set for eight *(counting)*—the four of us, Grandpa, Ellie, Pastor, and Mrs. Tyler. *(To audience)* "The four of us!" I like the sound of that. Mom, Dad, Travis, and me! Ellie is Travis's fiancée. Grandpa wouldn't miss this dinner. And Mom thought it would be

Before participants arrive, set a table in the front of the classroom with a tablecloth, fine china, glasses, silverware, and the like. Greet participants as they arrive. Suggest that parents and their children discuss what is missing from the table. When everyone has arrived, ask, **What is missing from the table?** *Allow time for participants to share their responses. Then say,* **People are missing from the table. What is a banquet without people?**

Ultimately, the reason for setting a fancy table and preparing a banquet meal is to enjoy it with other people. Without people, you have no banquet! In today's session, we will examine what is necessary in order to celebrate the Lord's Supper: what elements are necessary in order to celebrate the Lord's Supper; what we need to do in order to receive the Lord's Supper; and when we should receive the Lord's Supper. *Open with a prayer asking that the Holy Spirit would enlighten you as you study God's Word so that you may receive the Lord's Supper worthily. Then, invite a volunteer to read aloud the key verse for the day.*

nice to have Pastor here too. *(Setting wine and water crystal on table)* My great-grandmother brought this china and crystal over from Europe.

MOM: Use the best crystal.

JAMIE: Nothing but the finest. *(Places napkins in water glasses; stands in silence, admiring the table)*

MOM: *(Enters Stage R with floral centerpiece; places it on table)* And this! *(Joins JAMIE in a long look at the table)* Right, Jamie. Nothing but the finest for Travis. Home at last, safe and sound.

JAMIE: It will be good to have us all together again.

MOM: Like Grandma used to say . . .

JAMIE: *(To audience)* The one who had the china . . .

MOM: My cup runneth over!

Discuss:

1. **How is the meal in the drama like the Lord's Supper?** The family of God, all who possess saving faith in Jesus, gather together to receive the Meal. Jesus gives us nothing but the finest in the Meal—His body and His blood for the forgiveness of sins.

2. **Where in the Church's celebration of Communion do you see "nothing but the finest" at work?** Answers will vary. Most congregations bring out the finest for the celebration of the Lord's Supper. Bread is often placed on silver trays, and wine is poured into beautiful chalices. Also, the celebration of the Lord's Supper occurs during the Divine Service.

Looking for Answers

Discuss the questions that follow. If your class is large, divide into smaller groups so that everyone has a chance to share.

1. **Why is it so important to have bread and wine for the celebration of the Lord's Supper? See Matthew 26:26–28 and Luke 22:14–20.** Jesus instituted the Lord's Supper with bread and wine, which through His Word are also His body and blood. We set the table with the same elements that Jesus used to celebrate the first Lord's Supper.

2. **Who is worthy to receive the Lord's Supper? See 1 Corinthians 11:27–29.** We are not worthy to receive the Lord's Supper on our own merits. Instead, through faith in Jesus, we receive the Supper worthily, trusting in His promises that His body and blood are truly present in the meal, our sins are forgiven, and eternal life in Jesus is ours.

3. **How are we to examine ourselves before receiving the Lord's Supper?**

   a. **Psalm 38:18**—We examine ourselves by confessing our sin.

   b. **2 Corinthians 13:5**—We examine ourselves to see whether we have faith in Jesus Christ, confessing that He is truly present in the meal.

   c. **Ephesians 4:22–24**—We examine ourselves to see whether we plan, with the help of the Holy Spirit, to resist sin and temptation.

4. **Can I receive the Lord's Supper when my faith is weak? See Mark 9:24 and John 6:37.** Absolutely. Jesus instituted the Lord's Supper with the very purpose of strengthening our faith.

What Do You See?

1. **What do the bowls and plates in this painting tell about Holy Communion?** The bowls and plates are used in common. Calling the Sacrament Holy Communion reminds us that we share God's gifts to us with our sisters and brothers in the faith.
2. **Can you tell which disciple in the picture is Judas?** Judas stands by the door, clutching his cloak as if preparing to go out into the night in preparation for his betrayal of Jesus.
3. **How does the presence of Judas at the Last Supper serve as a warning for us today?** Judas attended that last meal with the disciples, but he still betrayed Jesus. Today, we, too, may fall away from Christ. However, He gives us the Lord's Supper to strengthen us in the faith.

The Holy Sacrament

Taking It Home

Students and their parents should spend 10 minutes or more this week discussing the following questions:

1. Describe a "nothing but the finest" meal your family celebrates. Why is it celebrated?
2. Talk about some of your family's prized heirlooms. How long have they been in the family? How did they end up in your home? Why are they so valuable to your family?
3. When has your "cup runneth over" with God's blessing?
4. How is celebrating Holy Communion like a family reunion?

Ask parents and students to review Questions 299–305 in *Luther's Small Catechism with Explanation*. These questions and answers focus on how to receive the Sacrament worthily.

Close with a prayer, thanking Christ for making us worthy through His suffering, death, and resurrection.

Divine Service

Key Verse

Oh give thanks to the Lord, for He is good; for His steadfast love endures forever! Psalm 118:1

Ask, **For what do we give thanks to the Lord?** *Allow time for participants to respond. Answers will vary.*

Tape newsprint sheets around the classroom. Write "What is the Divine Service?" on each sheet. Greet students and parents as they arrive, and hand them markers. Ask them to write responses to "What is the Divine Service?" on the newsprint. When all have arrived, review what the families wrote. Say, **The Divine Service is where God serves us with His Word and Sacraments. We then can worship God in response with prayer, praise, and thanksgiving. In the Divine Service, God strengthens and equips us for the week ahead. Today we will learn more about the gifts we receive in the Divine Service.** *Pray that by the Holy Spirit's power, your study of the Divine Service may become more meaningful for all participants. Invite a volunteer to read aloud the key verse for the day.*

Drama

After the Divine Service

(WADE and JOEL stand Center Stage. DAD is offstage. Each holds a Sunday bulletin.)

WADE: Well, Joel, what did you think?

JOEL: It was different.

WADE: Different, huh? What does that mean?

JOEL: I expected some of what we did. Some other things surprised me.

WADE: Like what?

JOEL: You sure sing a lot.

WADE: Yeah, I guess we do.

JOEL: And why did we keep standing up and sitting down? Sometimes I just wanted to stay sitting for a while.

WADE: I know what you mean. So what did you like?

JOEL: I liked the part where the pastor explained what is in the Bible. I understood what he meant. And I liked saying that prayer, the one that begins with "Our Father."

WADE: The Lord's Prayer.

JOEL: Right.

DAD: *(Enters Stage L)* Hey, guys.

WADE: Hi, Dad.

DAD: So how was church, Joel?

JOEL: I liked it a lot, Mr. Schultz.

WADE: Joel said he liked the sermon and the Lord's Prayer.

DAD: That's good. Can't go wrong with Pastor's sermons. And the Lord's Prayer, well, it's been around for two thousand years, and I don't know anyone who's tired of it.

WADE: What about all the singing, Dad? We were wondering why we sing so much.

DAD: I'm not really sure, but God's people have been singing for a very long time. The Book of Psalms in the Bible is a songbook for God's people. Maybe we've always sung just because we're so glad and so thankful. You know, sometimes you sing because you want to express what's deep inside.

JOEL: Did Jesus sing?

DAD: I think He did, Joel. Somewhere in the Bible it says that after Jesus and His disciples had celebrated the Lord's Supper, they sang a hymn.

WADE: One of those psalms, I bet.

DAD: Yeah, probably so.

JOEL: You know what I like about the Lord's Prayer, Mr. Schultz?

DAD: What's that?

JOEL: I liked how we kept saying "we" and "us" and "our." The prayer shows how we're in this together, doesn't it? It shows how we care about one another.

DAD: *(With a sense of wonder)* To be honest, Joel, I never thought about it that way. You're right, though. Good thought, buddy. I hope you come again next Sunday. Who knows, I may learn something! Now, let's get at those doughnuts. *(ALL begin to exit Stage R.)*

WADE: Say, Dad, about this standing up and sitting down . . .

DAD: "Holy aerobics," your grandpa calls it.

JOEL: "Holy aerobics"? *(All exit, laughing.)*

Discuss:

1. **How would you describe the Divine Service to someone who rarely attends?** Answers will vary. Accept all responses.
2. **What did you think of Joel's understanding of the Lord's Prayer?** Accept all responses. Lead class to see that God invites us, His children through faith and the waters of Baptism, to call upon Him as our dear Father.
3. **What does Joel's attending of the Divine Service tell you about Wade and his family?** Wade and his family believe worship is important, so important that they are eager to invite friends.

Looking for Answers

Discuss the following questions concerning the Divine Service. If the class is large, you may want to divide into small groups so that everyone has a chance to share.

1. **What is the Divine Service?** Accept all responses. If you did the opening activity with newsprint, you may want to refer to student and parent responses.
2. **Read the following portion of the introduction to *Lutheran Service Book*. Then answer the questions that follow.**

   Our Lord is the Lord who serves. Jesus Christ came into the flesh not to be served, but to serve and to give His life as a ransom for many. On the cross He offered Himself as a spotless sacrifice for the sin of the whole world. Through His perfect life and death, He accomplished forgiveness and salvation for all before the Father in heaven. By His empty tomb and ascension into heaven, He declared His victory over sin and death to all the world. Seated now at the Father's right hand, He graciously serves His Church with the gifts of salvation. On the Last Day, He will come again to gather His elect from every nation to celebrate the feast that will have no end.

Our Lord serves us today through His holy Word and Sacraments. Through these means, He comes among us to deliver His forgiveness and salvation, freeing us from our sins and strengthening us for service to one another and to the world. At Holy Baptism, He puts His name upon us, pours His Holy Spirit into our hearts, and rescues us from sin, death, and the devil. Through Holy Absolution, He pronounces His forgiveness again and again. With His holy Word, written in Scripture and preached into our ears, He daily proclaims His abiding love for us through all the joys and sorrows of life in this world. In His Holy Supper, He gives us His own body and blood to eat and drink as a priceless gift to nourish and strengthen us in both body and soul.

The Lord's service calls forth our service—in sacrifices of praise and thanksgiving to Him and in loving service to one another. Having been called, gathered, enlightened, and sanctified by the Holy Spirit, we receive His gifts with thankfulness and praise. With psalms, hymns, and spiritual songs, we joyfully confess all that God has done for us, declaring the praises of Him who called us out of darkness into His marvelous light.

Our song joins with the song of every saint from every age, the new song of Christ's holy people, declaring: "Worthy is the Lamb who was slain, to receive power and wealth and wisdom and might and honor and glory and blessing!" (Rev. 5:12). (*LSB*, p. viii)

a. **In what way did our God and Savior serve us in the past? In what way does He continue to serve His Church today? How will He serve His elect in the future?** Jesus came to give His life as a ransom for many. He lived a perfect life and died in our place a horrible death on the cross. By His empty tomb and ascension into heaven, He declared His victory over sin and death for all the world. Now He is seated at the right hand of the Father. From there, He graciously serves His Church with the gifts of salvation. On the Last Day, He will come again to gather His Church from every nation to celebrate the feast that will have no end.

b. **Jesus comes to us today through His Word and the Sacraments. What blessings does He serve to us through these means?** Through these means, He delivers His forgiveness and salvation, freeing us from our sins and strengthening us for service to one another.

c. **How does Jesus serve us through Holy Baptism?** He puts His name upon us, pours His Holy Spirit into our hearts, and rescues us from sin, death, and the devil.

d. **How does Jesus serve us through Holy Absolution?** He pronounces His forgiveness again and again.

e. **How does Jesus serve us through His Holy Word?** With His Holy Word, written in Scripture and preached into our ears, He daily proclaims His abiding love for us through all the joys and sorrows of life in this world.

f. **How does Jesus serve us through His Holy Supper?** He gives us His own body and blood to eat and drink as a priceless gift to nourish and strengthen us in both body and soul.

g. **Describe the service to which our Lord's service calls us.** The Lord's service calls forth our service—in sacrifices of praise and thanksgiving to Him and loving service to one another.

3. **The following are components of the Divine Service. Draw an arrow pointing down if the Lord is speaking to us in this part of the service and an arrow pointing up if we are speaking or responding to Him. Some may have both up and down arrows. You may need to review these components of the Divine Service from the hymnal.**

Invocation: Arrow down. God speaks to us the words that were first spoken at our Baptism, when we became His children: "In the name of the Father and of the Son and of the Holy Spirit."

Confession and Absolution: Arrow up. We confess our sins. Arrow down. God forgives us for Jesus' sake.

Hymn of Praise: Arrow up. We respond to the forgiveness we have received by praising God.

Readings: Arrow down. God speaks to us today through His Word.

Hymn of the Day: Arrow up. We respond to God's Word and anticipate hearing it more fully explained in the sermon.

Sermon: Arrow down. God speaks to us today as the pastor preaches from the Word of God.

Creed: Arrow up. We confess our faith in the triune God—Father, Son, and Holy Spirit.

Prayers: Arrow up. As the forgiven children of God, we offer prayers to Him.

Offerings: Arrow up. In praise and thanksgiving for the forgiveness of sins and eternal life Jesus won for us on the cross, we return a portion of that which He has given to us.

Preface to Communion: Arrow up. We give thanks to God for that which we are about to receive. We praise God with all the saints as we sing, "Holy, holy, holy!"

Lord's Prayer: Arrow up. We offer our prayers to God in the prayer He taught us.

Words of Institution: Arrow down. The words of Jesus when He instituted the Lord's Supper are spoken.

The Peace: Arrow down and arrow up. We share the peace of God that God first shared with us. We love because He first loved us.

Distribution: Arrow down. Jesus provides us His true body and true blood in, with, and under the bread and wine.

Prayer and Thanksgiving: Arrow up. We respond in joy and thanksgiving for the forgiveness of sins we have received in the Lord's Supper.

Benediction: Arrow down. God bestows on us His blessing. We are empowered by the Holy Spirit to share Jesus' love with others in the world.

4. **How would you describe the rhythm of the Divine Service as you review the arrows pointing down and the arrows pointing up?** God speaks first to us, and we respond to Him.

5. **Why is it important that the hymns we sing first and foremost reflect God speaking to us?** Again, the focus of Divine Service is on what God has done for us in Christ Jesus. Our hymns need to reflect Him and His Word.

6. **Review the Lord's Supper liturgy. How do we prepare ourselves to receive the Supper? How do we respond to the blessings we receive in the Supper?** We prepare ourselves to receive the Lord's Supper by confessing our sins and by receiving the faith-strengthening power of the Holy Spirit working through God's Word. We respond to the great blessings received in the Lord's Supper by giving God thanks and praise. We also respond to the great blessings by sharing His love with others.

What Do We See?

1. **What teaching is presented in this illustration?** Through the Sacrament of the Altar, believers receive forgiveness of sins, life and salvation, victory over sin, and an opportunity to participate in a public confession of faith and demonstration of unity.

2. **Which of the benefits of the Lord's Supper remind us that Holy Communion resembles, in a way, a huge family meal?** When we receive Christ's body and blood together with the bread and wine in the Lord's Supper, we celebrate the victory and blessings Christ has won for us and the unity we share with others by virtue of a common confession of faith in Jesus.

Receive the Benefits

3. **What important teaching regarding what is received in the Sacrament is not directly presented in this illustration?** In the Lord's Supper, together with the elements of bread and wine, Christ's very body and blood are truly present and received by participants in a mysterious way.

Taking It Home

Urge parents to spend 10 minutes or more this week discussing the questions below with their children. These questions will reinforce the truths discovered in this session.

1. Whom could we invite to worship with us? When will we do it?
2. How important is it that the rhythm of worship focuses first on God speaking to us?
3. How important is it that the words we speak, hear, and sing in worship come from the Bible?
4. What are the most important things you have learned about yourself, God, and the Lord's Supper during the past weeks?

Close with a prayer asking that the Holy Spirit would guide the students and their parents to come to the Lord's Table often.